Jenna Richardson

Copy rights published, 2016

Dedicated to my mother, Melissa, thank you—love you.

Biography, non-fiction

Introduction (from the author): I love the CBS show "The Big Bang Theory." Each character has something to give, a certain characteristic. I am a fan of Sheldon's eccentricities, Penny's spunk, and Raj's inability to talk to girls. I have been watching this show since I was 14 when it soon came on the air. I also enjoy seeing the cast change as time went on: it seems as if Penny's hair got shorter or Leonard got a little fatter. Sheldon, stayed the same however: which adds a little humor throughout, and this never gets old...Which is why I wanted to write this book. This coffee table book tells the biographies of all the young, apartment-sharing friends, with the new additional characters such as "Amy Farah Fowler and Bernadette" along the way. I know this show is popular among many generations. I also know that you will enjoy this book as much as I did writing it, and you will get a little knowledge along the way, like have you ever wondered where Jim Parsons got his start, or where Johnny Galecki was born? If so, get ready for an intergalactic, out of this world adventure—beam yourself up! –in memory of Leonard Nemoy (Star Trek).

Jim Parsons, or better known as: "Sheldon Cooper"

Born on March 24, 1973, in Houston, Texas, actor Jim Parsons rose to fame as Sheldon on the popular sitcom The Big Bang Theory. He studied at University of Houston. In 2001, Parsons completed his master's degree at the University of San Diego. He moved to New York City for a time after graduation where he found work in the theater. Parsons also landed roles on such television and film projects as Judging Amy and Garden State in 2004. In 2007, he began his successful run on The Big Bang Theory. Parsons has won Emmy Awards in 2010, 2011 and 2013 for his work on the show.

Born in Houston, Texas, on March 24, 1973, actor Jim Parsons is considered one of television's leading comedic performers. He has enjoyed tremendous popularity as scientific genius Sheldon Cooper on The Big Bang Theory. Parsons grew up in Houston with his sister, Julie, as the children of a school teacher and the president of a plumbing supply company. Parsons showed an interest in performing at an early age, beginning with studying the piano in kindergarten. A budding actor nearly from the start, he eventually developed his own scripts and staged productions at home.

Two-time Emmy Award and Golden Globe Award winner Jim Parsons was nominated for another Emmy Award in 2012 for his role as Sheldon Cooper in THE BIG BANG THEORY. His performance has also garnered him People's Choice Award nominations for "Favorite TV Comedy Actor" in both 2011 and 2012. In 2010, Parsons received the NAB Television Chairman's Award, which honors significant breakthroughs in television. Additionally, he recently received the Broadcast Television Journalists Association's award for "Best Actor in a Comedy Series" in their first-ever Critics' Choice Television Awards. He has twice been nominated for the TCA Award for Individual Achievement in Comedy, winning the prize in 2009.

This summer, Parsons is headlining the first Broadway revival of Mary Chase's Pulitzer Prize-winning play, "Harvey," in which he will star as

Elwood, the genial eccentric who claims to see a six-foot-tall white rabbit named Harvey.

Parsons made his Broadway debut in 2011, receiving a Theatre World Award for his performance as Tommy Boatwright in the revival of "The Normal Heart," starring opposite Ellen Barkin, John Benjamin Hickey and Joe Mantello. "The Normal Heart" received five Tony Award nominations and won the Tony for "Best Revival of a Play." It also won The Drama Desk Awards for "Outstanding Revival of a Play" and "Outstanding Ensemble Performance," and received a nomination from The Outer Critics Circle for "Outstanding Revival of a Play."

Parsons' additional stage credits include "The Castle" for the Manhattan Ensemble Theater, "The Countess" for the Globe Theater, and "The Tempest" and "As You Like It" for the Houston Shakespeare Festival.

Parsons is set to reprise his role as Tommy Boatwright in the film adaptation of "The Normal Heart," directed by Ryan Murphy. The film is scheduled to begin production later this year. Parsons' other feature film credits include scene-stealing roles in the "The Muppets," "The Big Year" and "Garden State." He also appeared in "School for Scoundrels," opposite Billy Bob Thornton, "Heights," opposite Glenn Close and James Marsden, and in the independent films "Gardner of Eden" and "The Great New Wonderful."

Parsons earned a Masters in Fine Arts degree from the Old Globe Theater/University of San Diego and a B.A. from the University of Houston. Born and raised in Houston, he now resides in Los Angeles. His birth date is March 24.

For more than a decade, Parsons has been in a relationship with art director Todd Spiewak. In speaking about their life together, Parsons said in 2013,

"I've never considered myself an activist. I've never considered my relationship with Todd to be an act of activism. Rather simply, it's an act of love, coffee in the morning, going to work, washing the clothes, taking the dogs [out]—a regular life, boring love."

Johnny Galecki, or better known as "Leonard Hofstadter":

Actor Johnny Galecki has made a name for himself by playing geeky guys, including long-running roles on the hit sitcoms Roseanne and The Big Bang Theory.

Actor Johnny Galecki was born in 1975 in Belgium, and moved to Illinois at the age of 3. In recent years, he's become the poster boy for adorable nerds on television. Acting on the small screen since age 12, Galecki has established himself as a prominent actor with two hit sitcoms: Roseanne, on which Galecki played Darlene Connor's awkward but devoted beau, David Healy, in the 1990s; and The Big Bang Theory, on which he began playing nerdy physicist Leonard Hofstadter in 2007.

John Mark Galecki was born on April 30, 1975, in Bree, Belgium, and raised in Oak Park, Illinois. His family relocated stateside when he was 3 years old—the same time that, according to Galecki, he knew he was going to be an actor. And it wasn't long before he was well on his way to accomplishing his dream. By age 7, Galecki had begun appearing in productions at Chicago's Goodman Theater. In 1989, he nabbed his first movie role in the family flick Prancer.

In 2011, Johnny Galecki received his first Emmy Award nomination as well as a Golden Globe nomination for his starring role as Leonard Hofstadter. Before starring in THE BIG BANG THEORY, Galecki was best known to television audiences for his role as David in the long-running comedy series "Roseanne," for which he won a Young Artist Award. His additional television credits include a recurring role in "My Boys" and guest appearances on "My Name is Earl." Last year, he was seen playing a "tougher" version of himself in the final season of "Entourage."

'Roseanne': Staying on the West Coast soon paid off for the teen: In 1992, he set foot on one of television's top shows at the time, Roseanne; Galecki was cast as David Healy, the boyfriend turned husband of Roseanne's snarky daughter, Darlene (played by Sara Gilbert), on the series. His character's sensitive and dorky demeanor captured audiences' hearts, we well as Roseanne Barr's—she decided to keep him on the show for the next five seasons.

Galecki credits the sitcom for honing his acting craft. "In many ways, Roseanne was my college," the actor said in a People magazine interview. After the series ended in 1997, Galecki continued to land minor acting gigs, including parts in the films I Know What You Did Last Summer, Bounce, Vanilla Sky and Hancock.

Galecki's feature film credits include "Hancock," opposite Will Smith, Charlize Theron and Jason Bateman, "The Opposite of Sex," "Bounce," "Happy Endings," "Vanilla Sky," "I Know What You Did Last Summer," "Suicide Kings," "Bookies," "Chrystal," "Playing Mona Lisa," "Bean" and "National Lampoon's Christmas Vacation." In 2011, he appeared in Andrew Niccol's "In Time" as Borel, the self-destructive best friend of Will Salas, played by Justin Timberlake. Galecki will next be seen playing band manager Terry Ork in the indie punk rock movie "CBGB," about the legendary New York club whose name stood for "Country, Blue Grass and Blues."

Galecki has numerous stage credits including the Tony Award-nominated Broadway play "The Little Dog Laughed," for which he received a 2007 Theater World Award for Outstanding Broadway Debut, "The Drawer Boy" and "Pot Mom" at Chicago's Steppenwolf Theatre, "The Member of the Wedding," for which he was nominated for a Joseph Jefferson Award, and "Galileo" at Chicago's Goodman Theatre, among others.

Born in Belgium when his father was stationed there while serving in the U.S. Air Force, Galecki was raised in Chicago, Ill. Currently, he resides in Los Angeles. His birth date is April 30.

In addition to bringing him industry recognition, The Big Bang Theory helped spice up Galecki's love life: For two years while filming the series, he secretly dated co-star Kaley Cuoco. In 2010, the couple amicably parted ways.

Galecki found love again a few years later with another actress, Kelli Garner. Unlike his clandestine relationship with Cuoco, it didn't take long for media outlets to report that Galecki and Garner were dating, as the couple began making regular public appearances early on.

Galecki is undoubtedly a rare breed of child star, growing up in the public eye without major dramas, except for those he's performed on screen.

Kaley Cuoco, or better known as, "Penny":

Actress Kaley Cuoco stars as Penny on the popular sitcom 'The Big Bang Theory.'

Born in California in 1985, actress Kaley Cuoco had her first taste of TV success with the family sitcom 8 Simple Rules in 2002. Five years later, she launched the next phase of her career with The Big Bang Theory, which has become one of television's most beloved comedies. Cuoco has also appeared in such films as Hop (2011) and The Wedding Ringer (2015).

Early Life and Career:

Kaley Christine Cuoco was born on November 30, 1985, in Camarillo, California, to parents Layne Ann Wingate and Gary Carmine Cuoco. She has a younger sister, Briana. Cuoco started working at a young age. She took up modeling as a child, and her first acting gigs were in commercials. Before long, Cuoco graduated to television work. She made guest spots on such series as Northern Exposure, 7th Heaven and My So-Called Life. Because of her career, Cuoco was homeschooled. She told People magazine that "I've never been to a regular high school."

Prior to THE BIG BANG THEORY, Kaley Cuoco was best known to television audiences for her role as Bridget Hennesy in the series "8 Simple Rules." Her other television credits include a recurring role on "Charmed," and guest appearances on "Complete Savages," "Prison

Break," "My So-Called Life," "Northern Exposure" and "Ladies Man." Cuoco starred in the cable movies "Fat Like Me," "Crimes of Fashion" and "The Hollow," and was seen in the miniseries "10.5." Her other television movie credits are "Alley Cats Strike," "Toothless," "Attack of the 50 Ft. Woman," "Growing Up Brady," and the miniseries, "Dean Koontz's Mr. Murder." Additionally, Cuoco lent her voice to the animated series "Brandy and Mr. Whiskers" and "Loonatics Unleashed."

Cuoco began her acting career at a young age, modeling and appearing in commercials. Her first TV role was in 1992's "Quicksand: No Escape" opposite Donald Sutherland. She landed her first feature film role at the age of 8 in "Virtuosity." Her other film credits include "Picture Perfect," "Can't Be Heaven" and "Lucky 13." She also appeared on stage in community theater productions of "Fiddler on the Roof" and "Annie."

Recently, Cuoco starred opposite Rob Lowe in the television movie "Untouchable: The Drew Peterson Story." On the big screen, she was seen in the 2011 family comedy "Hop" opposite James Marsden and Russell Brand. Cuoco will soon be seen in "The Last Ride," an independent film which has been screened at several film festivals throughout the country.

Cuoco is a gifted tennis player who also hikes, runs, rides horses, goes to the gym and spends time with her rescue dogs. She is involved in several charities, including EBMRF, Friends of Animals, the Humane Society, the Elisabeth Glaser Pediatric AIDS Foundation, Animal Avengers and PETA.

Currently, Cuoco resides in Los Angeles. Her birth date is Nov. 30.

Personal Life: Cuoco married Ryan Sweeting on December 31, 2013, but they announced they were divorcing in September 2015. Outside of work, Cuoco is an avid horse rider. She is also a former nationally ranked amateur tennis player.

Kunal Nayyar, or better known as, "Rajesh Koothrappali":

"The Big Bang Theory" star shares his Hollywood success story from cleaning toilets when he first came to America to becoming one of the most popular (and highest paid actors) in television.

In case you were wondering, yes, Kunal Nayyar's accent is real – and not simply because he's telling you so on the jacket to his recently published, bestselling memoir, Yes, My Accent is Real: And Some Other Things I Haven't Told You. In conversation, the 34-year-old – best known for playing Dr. Raj Koothrappali, the girl-shy, selectively mute, metrosexual astrophysicist with a thing for Halo, sweater vests, and the film oeuvre of Sandra Bullock on CBS' smash comedy, The Big Bang Theory – reveals that his accent isn't the only thing real about him. Raised in New Delhi, India where he played badminton, watched James Bond movies with his father, and got frequent nosebleeds, Nayyar came to America in 1999, with little more than a backpack and a common dream: to become a successful actor. As one of the highest paid actors on television today, Nayyar appears to be an object lesson in wish fulfillment, but a closer examination – the lean months of waiting tables and scrubbing toilets and auditioning endlessly for gigs he'd never get, then finally landing his "big break," playing an Iraqi terrorist on a weekly drama – shows Nayyar is more precisely the perfect example of wish earning. Quick witted, a touch goofy, always endearing, genuinely thoughtful and sincere, Nayyar may not know his "string theory" from his "double slit," scientific concepts Dr. Raj grasped before he was potty trained, but he is a charmed and charming cornucopia of real.

Including you, that's four members of the Big Bang Theory cast who have written a book. So are all of you actually geniuses, or is there any acting going on there?

(Laughs) I think the common consensus is that actors are either good or bad at acting, which is for all of the world to decide when they watch our films or television shows, but I think many people in the media and the public also think actors, in general, are probably not the smartest people. So when you write something insightful about your life, some people get very surprised.

So you are all geniuses!

Kunal's role in THE BIG BANG THEORY is his first as a regular on a television series, although he previously had a guest starring role on "NCIS," on the Network.

Recently, Nayyar completed production on the animated feature film "Ice Age: Continental Drift," which is slated for release in 2012. He also hosted "A Tribute to Nerds," at the 2011 Montreal "Just for Laughs" Comedy Festival. In an interview he stated, "(Laughs) To be completely honest, I'm very lucky and blessed to work with some incredibly talented artists. Four of the Big Bang cast have their own production companies now at Warner Bros, which is a trend in the entertainment industry these days. I think artists today want to be masters of their own destiny, as opposed to maybe 15 or 20 years ago, when actors would have to wait for the phone to ring to get a job. We like to make our own phone calls these days. We like to put together the writers and producers and cast to get our own work produced. Are we geniuses? (Laughs) I don't think so. But you can read our books and watch our shows and let me know!" In your book, you write very warmly of your father, who is apparently a wellspring of wisdom. Tell me about some of the things he's taught you.

Well, we don't get to choose our parents, right? You just wake up, you open your eyes, and your parents are standing there in front of you. Your mind is a blank slate, and you are 100% vulnerable to these people, and then you become a product of your upbringing. I was fortunate enough that my father instilled a lot of key values in me. Sometimes I struggle, of course, like everyone does, like my father did, but I know I'm better off for the wisdom he's shared with me. When I started writing some of those things down for the book, I became aware that there's a fine line between being preachy and being self-deprecating. Writing the book was about finding that balance. Ultimately, I could only write the book I had to write, and then I put it out there into the world with a good heart. I wrote down some things that helped me, and hope maybe it will inspire some other kid to live out his own destiny too.

Why was this the best time to write your book?

I've had the idea for a long time. See, my journey has been so intense and so rich – growing up in New Delhi and then moving to Portland, Oregon and then Philadelphia, and then paying my bills by becoming a waiter, like most actors do, and cleaning toilets too, then going off to auditions for some play in the basement of a computer store or something. When I started putting these stories together chronologically, I thought, "You know, if someone had lived this life, I sure hope they'd share it with me." As for why now? Well, obviously, it's entirely because of the success of The Big Bang Theory. I owe everything to that show. It's created a platform for me to communicate, to reach other people, hopefully to inspire them. Five or 10 years ago, when I was one of those wide-eyed kids coming to Hollywood with nothing but a big, silly dream, I'm not sure anyone would have listened to me, let alone read my book. I'm only 34 now, so I'm still not in a position to spew knowledge on someone, but I thought maybe I could humanize this journey a little bit. I think people have a kind of strange idea about what working in television is really like. It is totally amazing being on a show like The Big Bang Theory, but your struggles are, in a lot of ways, my struggles too. The circumstances may be a little different, but we all struggle in life, don't we?"

In today's celebrity culture, we tend not to perceive our heroes with much compassion, but as objects almost, which we'll put on a pedestal until we feel like watching them fall.

That seems to be a new phenomenon. It's the TMZ Culture, right? Fifteen, maybe 20 years ago, actors were revered in a way that maybe they're not today. Not that actors deserve reverence exactly, but they do deserve the same respect and courtesy any other human being does. Now, it's like, "Hey, let's take a photograph of that actor taking a giant, messy bite of his hamburger. Look how stupid he looks! He must be an idiot. Let's put it on YouTube!" Or let's catch Kunal at the airport after a 22-hour flight from India and ask him some inane question about politics and then show it on every news show around the world. It can be kind of brutal sometimes.

I don't have any questions about politics, but I promise you at least a couple of "inane questions."

(Laughs) Please, fire away! I love stupid questions!

It's said that where we are today is informed by everything we've done, everywhere we've been. You cleaned university toilets to pay your way through the early days of living in America. Is there a connection between polishing the porcelain throne and playing Dr. Raj or writing Yes, My Accent Is Real?

I think that when you have done something that maybe society thinks is ugly or dirty or somehow 'less than,' you realize that kind of work is actually a great equalizer in the game of life. I mean, I didn't clean toilets because I wanted to learn some great life lesson; I did it because I needed a job. Also, I hadn't cleaned toilets before I had that job. It's not that I grew up in a wealthy family, not at all, but even middle-class families in India have domestic help, so the toilets were cleaned for us. But in America, I had no domestic help. I had to learn how to do things I'd never done before, including cleaning toilets. It was that simple, really. I took the job because it paid better than minimum wage and no one else wanted to do it.

Still, it's not a ton of fun, cleaning up a bathroom after a Saturday night frat party...

No, that's true. It's disgusting. But I made it into a game, which is something I do, especially when I have to do something I don't really want to. Instead of focusing on everybody's poop and how disgusting my job was, I'd get down on my knees with my cleaning supplies and I'd start the job and sometimes I'd start wondering, "Hmm, that's interesting; what did they have for dinner?"

Life is a matter of perspective, isn't it?

Yes! Everything has the meaning that you give it. For me, cleaning toilets wasn't about, "Oh, this is so disgusting." Instead, it was, "Oh, this is awesome! Look how much money I'm making!"

There has been much made in recent years, and rightfully so, about Hollywood's need to hire more women and people of color and other minority groups. But I don't remember the "Hire People from India" movement, and yet we have wildly successful careers from you, Mindy Kaling, Aziz Ansari, Kal Penn, Anil Kapoor, Priyanka Chopra, Dev Patel. This strikes me as being truly significant, particularly seeing as how one of your first professional acting jobs was playing an Iraqi terrorist on NCIS!

Yeah, it makes me incredibly proud. It really does. I'm very proud of being Indian. I love wearing my ethnicity on my sleeve. I don't hide from it. It makes me incredibly proud to see Mindy doing such incredible work, not only because she is first-generation Indian, but also because she's a woman and she's doing extraordinary work in writing a powerful – and vulnerable and hilarious – female character. Aziz is an incredibly smart guy and his new Netflix series is amazing, and Priyanka has been a huge Bollywood star for many years and is now on her own hit series (Quantico) here in America. It's a good time, I suppose. I never really set out to break barriers myself. People try to drag me into discussions about typecasting, but my only response to that is, "Look, I'm an actor. All I want to do is act." It's almost impossible for anyone to get paid to do what they love in Hollywood, and I'm doing it. I never really wanted to take any gigantic political or social positions. When I was starting out, I just couldn't believe I actually had an acting job. Even today, I think the best thing I can do toward more Indian actors being hired is to be an excellent Indian actor, to do the best job I can, to create work I'm proud of.

Indeed. Probably the best political move any of us can make is to simply be who we are and let everybody else figure out what statements we're making.

Oh, that's well said. I do like that, yeah. You can put it as if I said that, okay?

Um, maybe… (Laughs) You just said that all you want to do is act, but that's simply not true, not anymore. You have the book. You've written a couple of plays. What else do you have up your sleeve?

I think I have a few things up my sleeve, but I try not to get too anxiety ridden about the future. In the past, that's driven me mad. But if you asked me about my immediate hopes and dreams, professionally at least, I'd tell you I have a very real, burning desire to do a movie in Hindi in India. It's doesn't necessarily have to be a big Bollywood thing, but maybe an independent movie, like Lunchbox or Monsoon Wedding or The Namesake. There's a beautiful script that I'm looking at that I would like to shoot in India this summer. I think that would be the most immediate step for me — to do a movie in India, where I'm from, in my native language.

Switching gears to an "inane question. . ."

(Laughs) Oh, excellent!

Several of your Big Bang cast mates are vegetarians or vegans. Do you get a lot of pressure to give up your beef stroganoff?

Wait. . .What? I don't even know which of the cast eats meat, or who doesn't eat meat. I maybe should pay attention to their lunch boxes! (Laughs) All I can say is: we're actors! If there's anything that actors are meticulous about, it's their diet and their skin products.

Absolutely! If I made my living in front of a camera, I'd be in the gym two-hours every day.

Exactly! I know people make fun of an actor's vanity, but if I don't take care of myself and I start looking really tired or old or horrible on screen, I might lose a job I really want. Actors get a lot of flack for being meticulous with their gluten-free diets and their animal-free skin products, but at the end of the day, it's our faces and bodies out there in front of millions of people for immediate judgment – and people are not shy about sharing those judgments. Everything we do is judged, so I think a lot of actors try to manage or control the things they can.

So no one's forcing animal rights pamphlets into your hand at work?

Look, I'm a Hindu, and I eat meat, so I'm the worst. I know this is true. Don't ask me if vegetarianism is good or bad! I'm the worst.

A few years ago, you married a truly beautiful woman, Miss India Neha Kapur. What's your secret? Is it that you're excellent at the game of badminton?

His theater acting credits include "Huck and Holden" at the Dahlia Theater in Los Angeles, for which Nayyar was awarded Best Male Lead in a Play on the West Coast by the Garland Awards, and "Love's Labour's Lost" at the Royal Shakespeare Company in Stratford-upon-Avon, England.

Nayyar also penned the critically-acclaimed play, "Cotton Candy," which continues to run in New Delhi.

Always a performer, Nayyar began acting in musicals and plays at a young age. After high school, he left India for the United States where he majored in business and took many acting classes at the University of Portland (Portland, Oregon). In his senior year, he was nominated as the best actor in his play, "The Rose Tattoo," and was given an invitation to the American College Theater Festival (ACTF) to compete in an acting competition, where he eventually won the Mark Twain Award for comic brilliance as well as a fellowship to the prestigious Sundance Theater Lab. He went on to receive his Masters in Fine Arts (MFA) from Temple University in Philadelphia.

"I really don't know. When Neha and I met, I was – and still am – in a stage of life where I felt very confident, comfortable in my own skin, and I think that can be very alluring to members of the opposite sex. I was sure of myself, without being cocky. I didn't have any demons in my head, so to speak. I had my feet on the ground. I think maybe she was attracted to those things. It certainly wasn't my looks. Or my height. Or my general physical attributes. (Laughs) It had to be something else! I should ask her, actually. I really have no idea what she saw in me. It definitely wasn't the whole acting thing. She's never seen the show."

Really?

Never. She's never seen it.

Maybe she loves you because of your really, really big, uh, book!

(Laughs) That's got to be it!

Your success has come very quickly. It wasn't much more than a decade ago that you came to Hollywood and landed what's become one of the biggest hits on television. What have you learned along the way?

The number one thing I've learned is that humility is key. You have to find a way, in your heart, to be genuinely thankful and sincerely humble for everything that has come your way. I've seen it snatched away from people so quickly in this industry —one day you're on top, and the next day you're out. One year, you make tons of money and you're driving a nice car and have a big house, and then the next year, your show gets cancelled and you can't book another job for five years. I've seen the rise and I've seen the fall. I guess all of this will come to an end for me too one day, but I don't want it to so I make sure to be on time, to be as kind as I kind, as humble as I can, to work as hard as I can. Those qualities will not ever go away, and they will serve me in whatever work I do. I think those are qualities every one of us would do well to develop in ourselves."

While in school, Nayyar played badminton and competed at state level in the region of North India. He is also a fanatical fan of cricket. He is said to have a killer shoulder shimmy. According to Nayyar, Wikipedia says his name means "one who sees beauty in everything" and it comes from a Himalayan bird known as the Painted Snipe.

He was born in London, England, and spent most of his younger years growing up in New Delhi, India. He currently resides in Los Angeles. Nayyar's birth date is April 30.

Simon Helberg as Howard Wolowitz and Nayyar as his best friend Raj. "I owe everything to that show," Nayyar says of The Big Bang Theory. "It's created a platform for me to communicate, to reach other people, hopefully to inspire them. Five or 10 years ago, when I was one of those wide-eyed kids coming to Hollywood with nothing but a big, silly dream, I'm not sure anyone would have listened to me, let alone read my book." (Photo: Courtesy CBS).

Mayim Hoya Bialik, or better known as, "Amy Farrah Fowler":

Big Bang Theory's' Mayim Bialik: There's Not Just One Way to Be Cool (INTERVIEW)

From child actor to mom to neuroscientist, Mayim Bialik tells us how she's stayed tenaciously grounded, hilarious, and nerdy after all these years.

 TODD AARON JENSEN NOV 5, 2014:

Like Dr. Amy Farrah Fowler, her alter ego on CBS's The Big Bang Theory, the top-rated comedy on network television, Mayim Bialik is smart, beautiful, jocular, plays the harp, and has a PhD in neuroscience. Which begs the question: is the 38-year old actress, thrice Emmy-nominated for her work on the smash series, even acting? "Well, I don't have a lab full of coked-up monkeys with nothing to lose," she quips, deadpan. "So yeah, I'm probably acting a little bit."

Bialik's witty retort, hardboiled without a trace of jest (and therefore twice as funny), is one her trademarks, well honed on NBC's early-'90s sitcom Blossom, where she played the adolescent voice of pragmatism in a home overrun by deeply flawed, but endearing male family members. Bialik's proficiency at tickling the nation's collective nerve is, she says, "a gift" from her extended family, many of them Jewish immigrants, who understood "the power and protection humor conveys."

In her regular column at Kveller.com, Bialik shares intimate, frequently hilarious stories about her eccentric bloodline, raising her two young sons, as well as vegan recipes, progressive parenting tips, "second-wave feminist ideas," she cracks, and helpful hints for detoxing your favorite simian after his latest blow binge. Okay, we might have made up that last one. As Big Bang enjoys an eighth season that is more-watched (and, arguably, funnier) than its first several, Bialik — who proudly identifies as "a character actress" — seems to have the world on a string. Even if her monkeys are out of control.

If history has taught us anything, it's that the future is usually not bright for child actors. You were in the Bette Midler film Beaches when you were 12, on a hit TV show when you were 14. How is it you avoided becoming another child actor casualty?

I come from kind of an old-fashioned family. My father always reminded me that all of my so-called fame could end in a heartbeat, so I'd better have other stuff that I was working on. After a few years of doing television when I was a kid, I knew I needed to take a break, that there must be a lot more to life. I wanted to go to college. I wanted to see the world.

Was acting something you always wanted to do?

Well, I'm actually considered a late bloomer for the entertainment industry, because I didn't start at 2 or 3. My parents weren't putting me in commercials when I was in diapers. But I come from a family that is very strong in its faith, and there was always a very strong sense of storytelling, a lot of humor. Comedy is tragedy plus time, right? We had that down, like a lot of close Jewish families do. When I was in elementary school, I was an awkward kid, kind of a weirdo, and my English teacher was a very stern and strict teacher, but she was also the Drama teacher. I love to make strict people like me, so I basically became really interested in Drama. I don't know that I was all that quote-unquote talented as a kid, but I was fearless. I wasn't hammy. I wasn't good at stealing the spotlight. But I had a very strange sense of humor and a very keen sense of being able to work a crowd, which must come from growing up in my very crazy, amazing family.

How is success different for you today than it was on Blossom, two decades ago?

First of all, I feel incredibly blessed. I had some lucky shots when I was a kid, and then I took some time off to travel and study and I became a mother, and when I auditioned for Big Bang Theory, I wasn't looking to be a full-time actress again; I just wanted to make enough money, literally, to pay for health insurance. Now I'm in this situation where I really love my job. It's relaxing. I'm a part of this incredible ensemble of actors with really great writing, and I'm as happy with one joke as I am with 20. That kind of perspective comes with what I'd like to believe is maturity of some kind. But the biggest changes are the off-camera ones. The publicity machine, the whole celebrity scene, that's really different today than it was 20 or 25 years ago.

Back then, if you were in Tiger Beat, that was a big deal, but now young women in the entertainment industry are expected to walk all of the red carpets and look a certain way – put on designer clothing, have plastic surgery, wear Spanx, and all that stuff. I think that would have been incredibly overwhelming and very stressful for me when I was a teenager. I mean, Seventeen refused to have me on their cover back then because I was too "unusual looking," even though I was on this very popular kids' show. Also, social media – the Internet, Twitter, Instagram, all that stuff – it's really changed the way people feel they relate to public figures. I think you need to be very aware these days of how much of yourself you show and in which ways. Its just part of the job now.

You've referred to yourself many times as a "character actress," which is often, at least historically, a euphemism for someone who is not classically "perfect" in appearance. What does that mean to you in terms of being a young woman in Hollywood?

Well, once you become aware that you don't look like a leading lady and maybe your voice doesn't sound like a leading lady, you learn to kind of go with it — if you're looking to get paid to perform. You learn to go after the cool, funky character parts, which is something I've always loved anyway. I was a weird kid. I was a weird teenager. I'm a weird adult. It's funny because in some sense I feel like maybe I'm less of an impressive actor, because I'm strange in real life. But yeah, "character actor" works for me.

I think it takes all types of actors. When I think of the character actresses that inspired me — and I mean in no way to compare myself — but they didn't look like most leading actresses and didn't act like them. Lucille Ball, Carol Burnett, Tracey Ullman, Bette Midler, those were the women that I really looked up to. And they got a lot of the best lines, too.

Beyond being very, very funny, Big Bang Theory has really normalized the cultural ideas of "nerds" and "geeks." That's a huge shift – that smart people, quirky people can also be kind of cool, that arguing string theory versus loop quantum gravity or obsessing over Leonard Nimoy doesn't mean you're somehow less-than.

Right. Absolutely! You know, I am a neuroscientist, so on a deeper level, I also think it's remarkable that we have a TV show that does not talk about diagnoses. Big Bang Theory does not talk about fixing or correcting people. It's a show about people who live with each other's quirks. Sometimes they're annoyed by them and sometimes they exploit them in ways that are funny as entertainment, but it doesn't really judge them, and that is a cool thing. Especially in the characters of Amy and Sheldon (the show's will-they-ever-couple, portrayed by Bialik and Emmy-winner Jim Parsons), we have a couple that is making a very significant and intimate relationship work on their terms. It's really interesting. I would argue it might be the longest running non-sexual relationship we've seen on television.

Except for Crockett and Tubbs, of course.

Of course!

On the show, your character has described Sheldon, her paramour, as "handsome, lanky, brilliant, with skin that has a pale, waxy quality."

And he's still lovable. I think that what we do with our show is we show how the other half really lives. I think many of us grew up with shows about beautiful people "hooking up" in various permutations. That's not most people's experience. And we also have a group of characters that, despite being teased, despite all of their difficulties, they have productive careers, they have a thriving set of friendships, they have a social life, they have girlfriends sometimes, and sometimes they don't. They have activities they enjoy and they're able to enjoy and share those activities. No one's telling them that they can't, and I think that's so important today. I know plenty of adults who play video games and Dungeons & Dragons. Those are good people. They're productive people and I think the notion that there's only one way to be cool… I just don't think it's even relevant any more, and I'm pretty happy about that."

Mayim began her successful acting career as a child and is best known for her lead role as Blossom Russo in the early-1990's sitcom, "Blossom." Throughout the 1980s and 1990s, she made guest appearances on some of television's most beloved shows, including "Murphy Brown" on the Network, "MacGuyver," "Webster" and "The Facts of Life." More recently, she appeared in the television series "Fat Actress" and "Curb Your Enthusiasm." Bialik's other television credits include recurring roles on "The Secret Life of the American Teenager" and "'Til Death."

On the big screen, Bialik played the young- Bette Midler in the film "Beaches," and appeared in Woody Allen's "Don't Drink the Water." She also portrayed 1960's activist Nancy Kurshan in the film "Chicago 8."

In 2000, Bialik earned a BS in Neuroscience and Hebrew & Jewish Studies from UCLA. She continued her studies at the University, earning a PhD in Neuroscience in 2007, with a doctorate examining Obsessive-Compulsive Disorder in adolescents with Prader-Willi syndrome. Bialik was a dedicated student leader at UCLA Hillel, starting and leading a Women's Rosh Chodesh group, chanting and blowing shofar for High Holiday services, and conducting and writing music for UCLA's Jewish a cappella group.

Bialik is a board member and co-founder and chair of Jewish Free Loan Association's Genesis branch, and is an avid student of all things Jewish. She is devoted to a lifestyle of attachment parenting, homeschooling, natural family living, vegan cooking, and even makes her own shampoo.

Born in San Diego to first generation Jewish American parents, Bialik now lives in Los Angeles with her husband and their two sons. She keeps a traditional Jewish home, caring for her boys with her husband. She is a frequent writer and speaker for a variety of Jewish groups around the United States. Her birth date is December 12. She can be followed on Twitter @MissMayim.-

Simon Helberg, better known as "Howard Wolowitz":

Prior to his work on THE BIG BANG THEORY, Simon Helberg was a regular on the sketch comedy show, "MADtv." He was featured in several other critically acclaimed television series, including "Studio 60 on the Sunset Strip," "Arrested Development" and "Reno 911!"

Simon Helberg is an actor and comedian who plays Howard Wolowitz on the hit sitcom 'Big Bang Theory.'

IN THESE GROUPS

FAMOUS PEOPLE IN TELEVISION

FAMOUS PEOPLE BORN IN UNITED STATES

FAMOUS NEW YORK UNIVERITY, TISCH SCHOOL OF THE ARTS ALUMNI

FAMOUS PEOPLE BORN IN CALIFORNIA

Show All Groups

Synopsis

Actor Simon Helberg started out with a few small TV roles before becoming a cast member of MADtv in 2002. He went on to guest roles on such shows as Reno 911! and Arrested Development. His next big break came with a part in Aaron Sorkin's Studio 60 on the Sunset Strip in 2006. The following year, Helberg joined the cast of Big Bang Theory as Howard Wolowitz.

Early Life

Born on December 9, 1980, in Los Angeles, California, actor Simon Helberg grew up in the entertainment industry. His father Sandy is an actor and writer and his mother Harriet is a casting director. In his early years, he was very interested in television. As he told USA Today, "I would come home and make sure I finished my homework every night by 8 o'clock, generally so that I could sit down and watch TV from 8 to 10." Helberg also enjoyed more active pursuits as a child, earning a black belt in karate by the time he was 10 years old.

As a teen, Helberg became involved in playing music. He explained to Conan O'Brien that he joined a rock band because "I thought it would make me cool." But the group had one problem—only Helberg was a skilled musician. The rest of the band couldn't really play. Helberg later made the switch to acting, enrolling at the Tisch School of the Arts at New York University. By the time he graduated in 2002, he had already landed a few bit parts.

'Big Bang Theory'

Helberg landed his first comedic role as a regular on the sketch show MADtv in 2002. He went on to make appearances on such sitcoms as Arrested Development, Joey, Reno 911! and played Alex Dwyer on the short-lived drama Studio 60 on the Sunset Strip. The show, created by Aaron Sorkin, debuted in 2006 and only lasted for one season. But this disappointment left Helberg free to tackle his most famous role to date.

In 2007, Helberg began playing aerospace engineer Howard Wolowitz on the sitcom Big Bang Theory. Howard is a friend of Leonard (Johnny Galecki) and Sheldon (Jim Parsons), two geniuses who are roommates. Kunal Nayyar plays their friend Raj and Kaley Cuoco is their neighbor Penny. This show about a group of brilliant yet socially deficient scientists quickly won over audiences.

During the show's run, viewers have watched Howard's transformation from wannabe ladies' man to husband of the equally bright Bernadette (Melissa Rauch). They also saw his character cope with the loss of his mother. Carol Ann Susi voiced Mrs. Wolowitz, who was mostly heard talking and yelling at Howard off camera. When Susi died in real life, the writers decided to have her character die on the show.

On the big screen, Helberg has appeared in the Academy Award-nominated films "A Serious Man" from the Coen Brothers, and "Good Night and Good Luck." His other feature film credits include "Old School," "For Your Consideration" and Judd Apatow's "Walk Hard: The Dewey Cox Story."

He also played the role of Moist in the Internet cult sensation, "Dr. Horrible's Sing-Along Blog."

Born and raised in Los Angeles, Helberg attended NYU's Tisch School of the Arts, where he trained at The Atlantic Theater Company. He is an accomplished pianist.

Currently, he lives in Los Angeles with his wife, Jocelyn. His birth date is Dec. 9.

Other Projects: Despite the demands of being on a hit sitcom, Helberg has found time to tackle other projects. He and his wife Jocelyn Towne worked together to bring We'll Never Have Paris to the big screen in 2014. The film was based on a time in their real-life relationship when the pair broke up. Helberg also appeared with Jason Ritter in Towne's 2013 dramatic film I Am I. He has lent his voice to several animated series as well, including Kung Fu Panda: Legends of Awesomeness.

Personal Life:

Helberg has been married to Jocelyn Towne since 2007. The couple have two children, daughter Adeline and son Wilder.

Melissa Rauch, better known as "Bernadette":

Melissa Rauch's television career spans such hit shows as "True Blood" and "The Office," as well as "Kath & Kim," "Dirty Sexy Money" and "Best Week Ever." Among her feature film credits are roles in "I Love You Man" and "Delirious."

Actress Melissa Rauch plays Dr. Bernadette Rostenkowski-Wolowitz on the hit sitcom 'Big Bang Theory.'

IN THESE GROUPS

FAMOUS PEOPLE IN TELEVISION

FAMOUS PEOPLE BORN IN UNITED STATES

FAMOUS PEOPLE BORN ON JUNE 23

FAMOUS PEOPLE BORN IN 1980

Show All Groups

Synopsis

Actress and comedian Melissa Rauch first wowed audiences with her one-woman show, The Miss Education of Jenna Bush, in 2005. She then appeared on such TV shows as Kim & Kath and True Blood before landing the role of Bernadette in the popular sitcom Big Bang Theory in 2009. Rauch also co-wrote and starred in the 2015 comedy The Bronze.

Early Life and Career

Born on June 23, 1980, in Marlboro, New Jersey, actress Melissa Rauch appears as Bernadette on one of TV's most beloved comedies Big Bang Theory. She dreamed of becoming an actress as a child. As she explained to Back Stage, she grew up attending an arts summer camp: "I remember being, like 7 or 8 and being on stage . . . and thinking, 'This is the best feeling ever.'" Rauch also loved performing stand-up comedy at the camp's talent shows.

Rauch pursued her love of performing during her college years. She studied her craft at Marymount Manhattan College, earning her degree in 2002. Rauch worked as a stand-up comedian and eventually starred in her own one-woman show The Miss Education of Jenna Bush. This fictional look at former president George W. Bush's daughter put Rauch on the map in the comedy world. It enjoyed runs in New York and Los Angeles. In 2005, the production received the award for outstanding solo show at the New York Fringe Festival. She co-wrote the play with Winston Beigel, her writing partner whom she met in college and later married. (Beigel now goes by the name Winston Rauch.)

'Big Bang Theory'

On the small screen, Rauch started out as a commentator on VH1's Best Week Ever. She then landed work on such sitcoms as Kath & Kim in 2008. In 2010, Rauch had a recurring role in the popular supernatural saga True Blood. Her biggest break to date came from a guest part on Big Bang Theory. Originally her character, Bernadette Rosenkowski, was also meant to make a brief appearance in the show's third season.

But the petite blond aspiring microbiologist won over audiences and became a series regular in the show's fourth season.

In the sitcom, Bernadette becomes involved with fellow scientist Howard Wolowitz (Simon Helberg), a friend of the show's two main stars Sheldon (Jim Parsons) and Leonard (Johnny Galecki). Working as a waitress to pay for her schooling, she also befriends Penny (Kaley Cuoco). Bernadette finished her Ph.D. and married Howard over the next few seasons. Rauch explained to the Huffington Post that playing a genius like Bernadette has been a learning experience. "There's science information that's given to me in each script that are things I never thought I would learn. . .My character did experiments with rhesus monkeys. I didn't even know that rhesus monkeys existed."

■ --Projects Beyond the 'Big Bang Theory'

In addition to her work on Big Bang Theory, Rauch has continued to perform live comedy with the Upright Citizens Brigade Theatre. She and some other comedians reenacted reality television in The Realest Real Housewives. Rauch has also lent her voice to a number of animated series, including Sofia the First.

On the big screen, Rauch and her husband co-wrote and co-produced the 2015 independent comedy The Bronze. Rauch also starred in the project along with Gary Cole and Sebastian Stan.

Rauch garnered critical acclaim for her award-winning portrayal of the former President's daughter in her one-woman stage show, "The Miss Education of Jenna Bush," which enjoyed runs in New York City and

Los Angeles, and was an official selection of the HBO U.S. Comedy Arts Festival in Aspen, Colorado. Rauch also co-wrote, directed and starred in the short film, "The Condom Killer," a film noir comedic satire.

Born and raised in Marlboro, New Jersey, Rauch received her BFA in acting from Marymount Manhattan College. Currently she resides in Los Angeles. Her birth date is June 23.

Manufactured by Amazon.ca
Bolton, ON